Punctuation Personified,

or

Pointing Made Easy

by Mr. Stops

Punctuation Personified,
or
Pointing Made Easy
by Mr. Stops

a facsimile of the 1824 edition

BODLEIAN LIBRARY, UNIVERSITY OF OXFORD

First published in 2004 by the Bodleian Library
Broad Street
Oxford OX1 3BG

ISBN 1 85124 194 9

Copyright © Bodleian Library, University of Oxford 2004

Designed by Dot Little. Cover design by Jessica Harvey.
Printed and bound by University Press, Cambridge

British Library Catalogue in Publishing
A CIP record of this publication is available from the British Library

A facsimile from two copies in the Bodleian Library:
Opie G 277 and Opie L 290(2). Frontispiece to the facsimile from
Sam Syntax's Description of the Cries of London, Opie P 153.

Introduction

PUNCTUATION, since its development in the fifteenth and sixteenth centuries into a form we recognize today, has attracted the attention of educators and grammarians bent on imposing rules and regulations governing its usage. The runaway success of Lynne Truss's recently published *Eats, Shoots & Leaves* is evidence that the subject is still a matter of concern to an awful lot of us: we all know what greengrocers' apostrophes are.

Six years before *Punctuation personified* was published, Cecil Hartley produced his *Principles of punctuation: or, The art of pointing familiarized.* This was explicitly for 'seminaries of education' and takes the form of questions and answers, initially between a tutor and his pupil. Though written for children, it is a serious schoolbook, and as such a far cry from the delightfully illustrated *Punctuation Personified*, which is more a picture book than an educational exercise.

Mr. Stops himself is an enchanting conceit, made as he is from punctuation marks, each of which is then given a human form (an exception is the apostrophe which is embodied as a mermaid).

From the severe legal figure of Counsellor Comma to the tumbling boys representing quotation marks, each 'stop' impresses itself pictorially, before the verses underneath explain its function and proper use.

The book was one of a series entitled 'Harris's Cabinet of amusement and instruction, consisting of the most approved novelties for the nursery,' which constituted John Harris's major contribution to juvenile literature. He took over the branch of the famous publishing house of John Newbery owned by Elizabeth Newbery in 1801, having worked for her as manager for some years. As is clear from the illustration of his shop in St Paul's churchyard, Harris continued Newbery's practice of selling patent medicines alongside books; but it was for children's books that he was primarily known.

> At Harris's, St. Paul's Church-yard,
> Good children meet a sure reward;
> In coming home the other day
> I heard a little master say,
> For every penny there he took
> He had received a little book,

With covers neat, and cuts so pretty,
There's not its like in all the city ...

Between 1801 and 1843 Harris and his son (also called John) produced many of the most attractive and entertaining children's books ever published, with an emphasis on fine illustration, often beautifully coloured by hand.

This facsimile of *Punctuation Personified* is made from two of the Library's copies, both of which are part of the vast collection of mostly eighteenth- and nineteenth-century children's books brought together by Peter and Iona Opie over many years. The entire collection – over 20,000 volumes – was acquired by the Bodleian Library in 1988. Today, it is one of the most important collections of early children's books and is consulted widely by specialists.

While Mr. Stops and Counsellor Comma may seem quaintly out of fashion as a way of teaching children to punctuate, the ability of the *dramatis personae* to amuse, delight, and indeed to instruct modern readers is a reflection of the book's enduring appeal and a testament to its author's modest brilliance.

The Facsimile

PUNCTUATION

Personified:

OR

POINTING MADE EASY.

BY

MR. STOPS.

LONDON:

J. HARRIS AND SON,

CORNER OF ST. PAUL'S CHURCH-YARD.

1824.

ROBERT'S first interview with MR STOPS.

Young Robert, could read, but he gabbled so fast;

And ran on with such speed, that all meaning he lost.

Till one Morning he met Mr Stops, by the way,

Who advis'd him to listen to what he should say:

Then, entring the house, he a riddle repeated,

To shew, WITHOUT STOPS, how the ear may be cheated.

MR. STOPS READING TO ROBERT AND HIS SISTER.

"Ev'ry lady in this land

"Has twenty nails upon each hand

"Five & twenty on hands & feet

"And this is true without deceit."

But when the stops were plac'd aright,

The real sense was brought to light.

COUNSELLOR COMMA, marked thus ,

Here counsellor Comma the reader may view,

Who knows neither guile nor repentance;

A straight forward path he resolves to pursue

By dividing short parts of a sentence;

As "Charles can sing, whistle, leap. tumble, & run",—

Yet so BRIEF is each pause, that he merely counts ONE.

ENSIGN SEMICOLON, marked thus;

See, how Semicolon is strutting with pride!

Into two or more parts he'll a sentence divide.

As "John's a good scholar; but George is a better;

"One wrote a fair copy; the other a letter:"

Without this gay ensign we little could do;

And when he appears we must pause & count TWO

A COLON, marked thus :

The colon consists of two dots, as you see;

And remains within sight whilst you count one, two, three:

Tis us'd where the sense is complete, tho but part

Of the sentence you're reading, or learning by heart.

As 'Gold is deceitful: it bribes to destroy'.

'Young James is admired: he's a very good boy:'

Before you read more
Stop; and count four.
1, 2, 3, 4.

A PERIOD or FULL STOP,

marked thus .

The full-fac'd gentleman here shown

To all my friends, no doubt, is known;

In him the PERIOD we behold,

Who stands his ground whilst four are told;

And always ends a perfect sentence,

As "Crime is follow'd by repentance".

THE INTERROGATIVE POINT?

What little crooked man is this?

He's call'd INTERROGATION, Miss:

He's always asking this & that,

As "What's your name? Whose dog is that?"

And for your answer, he will stay

While you, One, Two, Three, Four, can say.

THE EXCLAMATION POINT !

or Note of Admiration.

This Youth, so struck with admiration,

Is of a wondering generation,

With face so long, and thin and pale,

He cries, "Oh! what a wonderous tale!"

While you count four, he stops, and then,

Admiring! he goes on again.

An Apostrophe '

The comma, plac'd as here you see,

From the word LOV'D has snatch'd a letter;

It bears the name APOSTROPHE: —

And, perhaps, you can't contrive a better.

In poetry 'tis chiefly found,

Where sense should coincide with sound.

A DASH– · CIRCUMFLEX⌃ BREVE ⌣ DIÆRESIS ·· HYPHEN

ACUTE ACCENT ⁄ GRAVE ACCENT ⁀ PARENTHESIS ( )

A DASH & a CIRCUMFLEX here form a hat;

A BREVE serves to mark out the face;

DIÆRESIS, too, & the HYPHEN come pat,

As a breast & a neck in their place:

The arms are the ACCENTS, both GRAVE & ACUTE,

And for legs the PARENTHESIS nicely may suit.

A CARET, marked thus Λ.

If you a letter are inditing

And make an error in your writing,

By leaving out a word, or two,

The CARET may be us'd by you;

As "This ^new book to Charles I send,

And hope to please ^my dearest friend".

A SECTION, marked thus §.

This Gentleman of deep reflections,

Divides a subject into Sections;

Ideas ranging under heads,

As gardens are laid out in beds;

That o'er the whole the eye may move,

Survey the plan, & then approve.

A PARAGRAPH ¶.

The PARAGRAPH, which here you view,

Always announces something new;

Distinct from what was read before,

As is the water from the shore.

This mark in Scripture oft is found,

As thriving best on sacred ground.

A QUOTATION " "

Two commas standing on their heads,

Their orders are obeying;

Two others, risen from their beds,

Their best respects are paying;

These four are ushers of much use,

As they great authors introduce.

BRACKETS or CROTCHETS [] BRACE } ELLIPSIS ___

PARALLELS || OBELISK † DOUBLE DAGGER ‡ ASTERISK *

These BRACKETS some words may enclose, without doubt;

The BRACE sev'ral lines will unite;

ELLIPSIS is us'd where we letters leave out,

As k-t may be read for a knight.

The PARALLELS, OBLISK, & DAGGERS we find,

Like the ASTERISK only for refrence design'd.

AN INDEX HAND

The INDEX, or hand, is intended to shew

Some sentence deserving attention;

And this the young reader will probably know,

When one thing we venture to mention:

Wherever our book may appear in the shops,

A finger will point out the words, "MIND YOUR STOPS."